AF480671

ALTRUISTIC ALCHEMY

TRANSFORMING LIVES THROUGH GIVING

DR. MINAKSHI BANSAL

DEDICATION

*To those who dare to dream, strive for greatness,
and embrace the power of their own potential.*

❦❦❦

Contents

Contents

Prayer

"Om Poornamadah Poornamidam Poornaat Poornamudachyate,
Poornasya Poornamaadaya Poornamevavashishyate"
"Om Shantih, Shantih, Shantih"

*The literal interpretation of this mantra is: That which is Absolute,
This which is Absolute, Absolute arises from Absolute, If Absolute is
removed from Absolute, Absolute remains*

*This mantra is a reminder of the fundamental truth that all of
existence is rooted in the Absolute. It is a reminder that the Absolute is
the source of all that is, and that it is ever-present, even when all else
is taken away. It is a reminder of the peace that comes from
understanding and accepting this truth.*
Om Peace, Peace, Peace.

About The Author

Dr. Minakshi Bansal, born in the bustling metropolis of Delhi, India, has led a life steeped in artistry, scholarly pursuit, and an unwavering commitment to societal betterment. Following her marriage, she relocated to Ahmedabad, Gujarat, where she has since blossomed into a multifaceted beacon of inspiration for many. Dr. Minakshi is not only recognized as a gifted artist in the realm of Fine Arts but also as an esteemed author, a devoted social worker and a dedicated research scholar in Psychology. Her journey, marked by a profound dedication to elevating those around her, especially the downtrodden and underprivileged children of society, is a testament to her deep-seated belief in the transformative power of engagement and empathy.

From her earliest days, Minakshi was distinguished by an insatiable appetite for reading. Her literary universe was inhabited by characters and narratives that spanned ethical tales, motivational and inspirational stories, and the mythic parables imbued with life lessons. This voracious reading habit was not merely for personal edification but was driven by a desire to distill and disseminate the essence of these narratives to foster the development of students and peers alike. She was particularly captivated by the lives and teachings of historical figures and spiritual leaders such as Adi Shankaracharya, Swami Vivekananda, Dr. APJ Abdul Kalam, Mahamana Pandit Madan Mohan Malviya, Mahatma Gandhi, Sardar Vallabhai Patel, and Vinoba Bhave, among others. Their philosophies and life stories fueled her ambition to embody their ideals of resilience, selflessness, and relentless pursuit of knowledge.

Dr. Minakshi's academic and practical engagement with psychology has been equally noteworthy. As a research scholar, her focus has been on exploring the intricate tapestry of the human psyche, aiming to unlock the potential for psychological well-being and societal harmony. Her scholarly work is complemented by her active involvement in social work, where she employs her academic insights to make tangible differences in the lives of the underprivileged. Her endeavours in social work are characterized by an innovative approach that combines traditional wisdom with contemporary psychological practices to address the multifaceted challenges faced by these communities.

Her artistic talents, another facet of her diverse capabilities, are not merely a personal passion but also serve as a medium through which she communicates and connects with others. Her art, rich in symbolism and emotional depth, reflects her philosophical inquiries and social concerns, offering viewers a glimpse into the breadth of her intellect and the depth of her compassion.

In addition to her contributions to the arts and social sciences, Dr. Minakshi has embraced the healing arts of Pranic Healing, mastering the techniques developed by Master Choa Kok Sui. This practice, which focuses on the manipulation of Prana or life energy to heal the body and aura, has been both a personal journey of discovery and a means through which she extends her healing touch to others. Her proficiency in Pranic Healing is complemented by her advocacy and teaching of various forms of meditation aimed at rejuvenation, personal betterment, and the cultivation of harmony within individuals and communities alike.

Dr. Minakshi's life is a narrative of relentless pursuit, not just of personal achievement but of the upliftment and empowerment of society at large. Her diverse interests and talents—spanning the arts, literature, psychology, and the healing practices—converge on a singular path of service. She embodies the spirit of the luminaries who inspired her, channelling their legacy through her actions and teachings. Through her books, art, and social initiatives, she continues to inspire a new generation to embark on their own journeys of self-discovery, resilience, and altruism.

Her commitment to social betterment, particularly her focus on uplifting underprivileged children, reflects a deep understanding of the transformative potential of education and personal development. By integrating her knowledge of psychology, her artistic sensibilities, and her healing practices, Dr. Bansal has developed a holistic approach to social work that addresses both the immediate needs and the long-term well-being of the communities she serves.

As an author, Dr. Minakshi's writings offer a blend of inspirational insights, practical wisdom, and reflective contemplations drawn from her extensive reading and life experiences. Her books serve as a guide for those seeking to navigate the complexities of life with grace, resilience, and purpose. Through her narratives, she extends an invitation to her readers to explore the depths of their own potential and to contribute meaningfully to the collective well-being of society.

In Dr. Minakshi Bansal, we find a remarkable synthesis of the artist, the scholar, the healer, and the social activist. Her life's work stands as a beacon of hope and a source of inspiration for individuals seeking to make a difference in the world. Her story is a compelling reminder of the power of individual action, rooted in compassion and driven by a profound commitment to the betterment of humanity. Dr. Minakshi's legacy is not just in the tangible outcomes of her efforts but in the enduring spirit of inquiry, empathy, and service that she embodies.

ᑭᑭᑭ

Preface

In the heart of Varanasi, a city steeped in spirituality and ancient wisdom, I found myself pondering the essence of giving. Surrounded by the rhythmic chants of prayers, the fragrant smoke of incense, and the gentle lapping of the Ganges River, I embarked on a journey to explore the transformative power of altruism. This book is a culmination of that journey, a testament to the profound impact that giving can have on our lives and the world around us.

As a woman who has witnessed both the depths of human suffering and the heights of human compassion, I have come to believe that giving is not merely an act of charity but a sacred practice, an alchemical process that transmutes our hearts and souls, enriching our lives in ways we could never have imagined. It is a force that transcends boundaries of class, race, and religion, uniting us in a common bond of empathy and compassion. Through personal anecdotes, reflections, and insights gleaned from a diverse range of sources, I invite you to join me on this exploration of altruistic alchemy, discovering the myriad ways in which giving can transform our lives and the world we inhabit.

My own journey with giving began at a young age, witnessing the selfless acts of my parents and grandparents, who instilled in me the importance of sharing what we have with others. Growing up in Varanasi, a city where generosity is deeply embedded in the cultural fabric, I was surrounded by countless examples of individuals who dedicated their lives to serving others. From the humble rickshaw puller who donated a portion of his meager earnings to charity, to the wealthy merchant who established a school for underprivileged children, I saw firsthand the transformative power of giving.

As I embarked on my own career and life journey, I continued to witness the profound impact of giving in various contexts. I saw how a simple act of kindness could brighten someone's day, how volunteering could empower individuals and communities, and how philanthropic endeavors could create lasting change. I also experienced the transformative power of giving in my own life, as it brought me greater joy, fulfillment, and a deeper sense of connection to the world around me.

Through my research and personal experiences, I have come to understand that giving is not merely an act of charity but a fundamental human need. It is hardwired into our DNA, a natural expression of our interconnectedness and our desire to contribute to the well-being of others. When we give, we tap into a wellspring of compassion and empathy, activating a neural circuitry that floods our brains with feel-good hormones like oxytocin and dopamine. This not only makes us feel good but also motivates us to continue giving, creating a positive feedback loop that reinforces our altruistic tendencies.

Giving is not just about donating money or resources; it encompasses a wide range of behaviors, from offering a helping hand to a stranger to advocating for social justice. It is a mindset, a way of being that prioritizes the well-being of others and seeks to create a more equitable and compassionate world.

In the following pages, we will explore the many facets of giving, delving into its psychological, social, and spiritual dimensions. We will examine the various forms that giving can take, from individual acts of kindness to large-scale philanthropic initiatives. We will also discuss the challenges and obstacles that can hinder our ability to give, offering practical strategies for overcoming them and cultivating a more generous spirit.

Through personal anecdotes, case studies, and insights from experts in various fields, we will uncover the transformative power of giving in all its glory. We will see how giving can strengthen communities, heal relationships, and promote personal growth and well-being. We will also explore the role of giving in addressing global challenges such as poverty, inequality, and environmental degradation.

This book is not a prescriptive guide, but rather an invitation to embark on your own unique journey of giving. It is my hope that through these pages, you will be inspired to explore the myriad ways in which you can make a positive difference in the world. Whether it is through volunteering your time, donating to a worthy cause, or simply offering a kind word or gesture, every act of giving has the power to transform lives, including your own.

ϼϼϼ

ONE

THE MAGIC OF ALTRUISM

Altruism, the selfless concern for the well-being of others, often regarded as a magical force, can transform lives and communities in profound ways. When individuals engage in acts of altruism, they create a ripple effect that extends far beyond the initial act, touching numerous lives and fostering a sense of interconnectedness and compassion. The magic of altruism lies in its ability to generate positive change not only for the recipients but also for the givers, creating a cycle of generosity and kindness that can enhance overall well-being and strengthen societal bonds.

Altruism begins with empathy, the ability to understand and share the feelings of others. This fundamental human trait allows individuals to connect with others on a deep emotional level, fostering a sense of shared humanity. Empathy acts as the catalyst for altruistic behavior, motivating individuals to take action to alleviate the suffering of others. When people witness the struggles or hardships of those around them, their empathetic response often drives them to offer support, assistance, or comfort. This initial spark of empathy ignites the transformative power of altruism, setting in motion a chain reaction of positive actions and reactions.

One of the most compelling aspects of altruism is its impact on mental and emotional well-being. Numerous studies have shown that engaging in altruistic behavior can lead to increased happiness, reduced stress, and a greater sense of purpose in life. When individuals help others, their brains release endorphins, often referred to as "helper's high," which produce feelings of joy and satisfaction. This natural reward system reinforces altruistic behavior, encouraging individuals to continue performing acts of kindness. Moreover, altruism can provide a sense of meaning and fulfillment, as individuals feel they are contributing to something greater than themselves, fostering a deeper connection to their community and society.

The benefits of altruism extend beyond the individual to the broader community. Acts of altruism can strengthen social bonds, creating a more cohesive and supportive society. When individuals engage in selfless acts, they build trust and goodwill within their communities, encouraging others to reciprocate and participate in similar behaviors. This collective engagement fosters a sense of unity and collaboration, as people come together to address common challenges and support one another. In times of crisis or adversity, altruism becomes a vital resource, as communities rally together to provide aid and assistance to those in need.

Altruism also plays a crucial role in shaping societal values and norms. When individuals consistently engage in selfless behavior, they set an example for others, promoting a culture of generosity and compassion. This cultural shift can lead to systemic changes, as societies prioritize the well-being of all their members and strive to create more equitable and just environments. For instance, community-led initiatives to support marginalized or vulnerable populations can inspire broader social movements, driving policy changes and fostering greater inclusivity and fairness. In this way, the magic of altruism lies in its ability to inspire and catalyze lasting societal transformation.

Another remarkable aspect of altruism is its capacity to bridge divides and foster understanding between diverse groups. In a world often marked by division and conflict, acts of altruism can serve as powerful tools for reconciliation and peacebuilding. When individuals from different backgrounds come together to help one another, they break down barriers and build relationships based on mutual respect and empathy. These connections can lead to greater tolerance and acceptance, as people recognize their shared humanity and common goals. Altruism, therefore, has the potential to create more harmonious and inclusive societies, where diversity is celebrated, and differences are respected.

The transformative power of altruism is also evident in its ability to inspire innovation and creativity. When individuals are motivated by a desire to help others, they often develop innovative solutions to address complex social issues. This drive for positive change can lead to the creation of new technologies, programs, and initiatives that improve the quality of life for countless people. For example, social entrepreneurs who prioritize altruistic goals often develop groundbreaking products and services that address pressing needs in their communities. By harnessing the magic of altruism, these innovators can create lasting and meaningful impact, demonstrating the profound potential of selfless action.

Furthermore, altruism can play a vital role in personal development and growth. Engaging in acts of kindness and compassion can help individuals develop essential life skills, such as communication, problem-solving, and leadership. By working to support others, individuals learn to navigate complex social dynamics, manage conflicts, and build collaborative relationships. These skills are invaluable in both personal and professional contexts, contributing to overall success and well-being. Additionally, altruistic behavior can foster resilience and emotional intelligence, as individuals learn to cope with challenges and setbacks while maintaining a positive and empathetic outlook.

The magic of altruism is not limited to grand gestures or significant acts of charity. Everyday acts of kindness and generosity can have a profound impact on both the giver and the recipient. Simple actions, such as offering a helping hand, listening to someone in need, or sharing a smile, can create moments of connection and joy that brighten the lives of those involved. These small acts of kindness accumulate over time, creating a culture of compassion and generosity that permeates all aspects of life. By embracing the magic of altruism in their daily interactions, individuals can contribute to a more caring and supportive world.

Altruism also has the potential to transform relationships, fostering deeper connections and greater intimacy between individuals. When people prioritize the well-being of others, they build trust and loyalty, creating stronger and more meaningful bonds. This focus on selflessness and compassion can enhance relationships with family, friends, and colleagues, leading to greater overall satisfaction and happiness. Additionally, altruism can help individuals navigate conflicts and disagreements, as they approach these situations with empathy and a genuine desire to understand and support one another.

In the realm of education, altruism can play a transformative role in shaping the values and attitudes of future generations. By teaching children and young adults the importance of empathy, compassion, and selflessness, educators can foster a culture of giving and community-mindedness. Service-learning programs and community involvement initiatives provide students with opportunities to engage in altruistic behavior, helping them develop a sense of social responsibility and civic engagement. These experiences can have a lasting impact, influencing the way young people view their role in society and inspiring them to become active contributors to the common good.

The magic of altruism is also evident in its ability to promote physical health and well-being. Research has shown that engaging in acts of kindness can lead to numerous health benefits, including lower blood pressure, reduced stress, and improved immune function. These positive effects are likely due to the reduction in stress and the increase in positive emotions associated with altruistic behavior. By prioritizing the well-being of others, individuals can also improve their own health, creating a virtuous cycle of giving and well-being.

Moreover, altruism can serve as a powerful antidote to the feelings of isolation and disconnection that are increasingly prevalent in modern society. In a world where people are often separated by physical distance and digital barriers, acts of altruism can create meaningful connections and foster a sense of belonging. By reaching out to help others, individuals can combat loneliness and build supportive networks that enhance their overall quality of life. These connections are essential for mental and emotional well-being, providing a source of support and comfort in times of need.

The magic of altruism also extends to the natural world, as individuals engage in selfless acts to protect and preserve the environment. Environmental altruism, such as conservation efforts, sustainable living practices, and advocacy for climate action, demonstrates a deep concern for the well-being of future generations and the planet. These efforts can lead to significant positive changes, such as the preservation of natural habitats, the reduction of pollution, and the promotion of sustainable development. By prioritizing the health of the planet, individuals can contribute to a more sustainable and equitable world for all.

In the workplace, altruism can enhance organizational culture and performance. When leaders and employees prioritize the well-being of their colleagues and the community, they create a positive and supportive work environment. This focus on altruism can lead to increased job satisfaction, higher levels of engagement, and improved team dynamics. Organizations that embrace altruistic values are also more likely to attract and retain top talent, as employees are drawn to companies that prioritize social responsibility and ethical behavior. By fostering a culture of giving and compassion, businesses can achieve greater success and make a positive impact on society.

The transformative power of altruism is also evident in its ability to inspire hope and resilience in the face of adversity. During times of crisis, acts of selflessness and compassion can provide a beacon of light, offering comfort and support to those in need. Whether through disaster relief efforts, community support programs, or individual acts of kindness, altruism can help individuals and communities navigate challenging times with strength and grace. These acts of giving not only provide immediate relief but also foster a sense of solidarity and hope, reminding people of their capacity to overcome difficulties together.

Ultimately, the magic of altruism lies in its ability to create a more compassionate, connected, and caring world. By prioritizing the well-being of others, individuals can contribute to a culture of generosity and kindness that benefits everyone. This focus on altruism can lead to profound personal growth, stronger communities, and a more just and equitable society. As individuals embrace the magic of altruism, they unlock the potential for transformative change, both within themselves and in the world around them. By cultivating empathy, practicing selflessness, and engaging in acts of kindness, individuals can harness the magic of altruism to create a brighter and more hopeful future for all.

♥♥♥

*Giving is not a mere transaction; it is an act of love
that transforms both the giver and the receiver.
When we open our hearts and share our resources,
we create a ripple effect of compassion that can heal
and uplift entire communities.*

ᐅᐅᐅ

TWO

THE JOY OF GIVING

The joy of giving is a profound and enriching experience that transcends the act itself, touching the lives of both the giver and the recipient. At its core, giving is an expression of empathy, compassion, and love, qualities that form the bedrock of human connection and community. The act of giving, whether it be time, resources, or support, creates a sense of fulfillment and joy that is both immediate and lasting. This joy is not only a fleeting emotion but also a profound state of being that can transform one's perspective on life and relationships.

When individuals give selflessly, they experience a sense of purpose and satisfaction that is difficult to achieve through other means. This satisfaction arises from knowing that one's actions have positively impacted another person's life. The immediate joy of seeing a smile, receiving heartfelt thanks, or witnessing the improvement in someone's situation provides an unparalleled sense of accomplishment. This feeling of purpose and contribution is a key component of the joy of giving, as it affirms the giver's ability to make a difference in the world.

The act of giving also triggers a cascade of positive emotions and physiological responses that contribute to overall well-being. Studies have shown that acts of kindness and generosity activate the brain's reward centers, releasing endorphins and other feel-good chemicals. This phenomenon, often referred to as the "helper's high," creates a sense of euphoria and contentment. Moreover, giving can reduce stress, lower blood pressure, and enhance overall mental health. These physiological benefits are a testament to the deep connection between altruism and personal well-being, illustrating that the joy of giving is rooted in our biology.

Beyond the immediate emotional and physiological benefits, the joy of giving fosters a deeper sense of connection and community. When individuals engage in acts of generosity, they build bonds of trust and mutual respect with others. These bonds are the foundation of strong, supportive communities where people look out for one another and work together for the common good. The sense of belonging that arises from being part of a giving community enhances social cohesion and resilience, making it easier for individuals and groups to navigate challenges and celebrate successes together.

The joy of giving is also reflected in the personal growth and transformation that often accompanies altruistic behavior. When individuals give, they step outside of their own needs and concerns, broadening their perspective and developing greater empathy and compassion. This shift in focus can lead to increased emotional intelligence and self-awareness, as givers learn to understand and respond to the needs of others. Additionally, the experience of giving can build confidence and a sense of agency, as individuals recognize their capacity to effect positive change in the world.

One of the most beautiful aspects of the joy of giving is its ability to create a ripple effect, inspiring others to act with generosity and kindness. When people witness acts of giving, they are often moved to emulate this behavior, creating a chain reaction of positive actions. This ripple effect can transform entire communities, fostering a culture of generosity and compassion that permeates every aspect of life. The joy that arises from giving is thus not limited to the individual but can spread throughout a network of relationships, amplifying its impact and creating a more caring and supportive environment.

The joy of giving is not confined to grand gestures or significant acts of charity; it can be found in the small, everyday acts of kindness that brighten someone's day. Simple actions like offering a helping hand, sharing a meal, or listening to someone in need can create moments of connection and joy that are deeply meaningful. These small acts of giving remind us that generosity is accessible to everyone, regardless of their circumstances. They demonstrate that the capacity for kindness is within us all and that even the smallest act of giving can have a profound impact.

Giving also has the power to heal and bring joy to the giver in times of personal hardship or struggle. Engaging in acts of kindness can provide a sense of purpose and perspective, helping individuals cope with their own challenges. By focusing on the needs of others, givers often find relief from their own worries and a renewed sense of hope and resilience. This healing aspect of giving underscores its transformative power, as it can bring light and joy even in the darkest of times.

Furthermore, the joy of giving extends to relationships, enhancing bonds and fostering deeper connections. When individuals give to those they care about, they strengthen their relationships through acts of love and support. This can lead to greater trust, intimacy, and mutual appreciation, creating a foundation for lasting and meaningful connections. The joy that arises from giving in relationships is a testament to the power of generosity to nurture and sustain the bonds that are most important in our lives.

In the context of family life, the joy of giving plays a crucial role in shaping values and nurturing a culture of empathy and compassion. When families prioritize giving, they teach children the importance of generosity and community-mindedness from a young age. Family activities that involve giving, such as volunteering together or supporting charitable causes, can create lasting memories and instill a sense of social responsibility. These experiences not only bring joy to the family but also lay the groundwork for future generations to carry forward the values of kindness and altruism.

The workplace is another arena where the joy of giving can have a significant impact. When organizations embrace a culture of giving, they create a positive and supportive work environment that benefits both employees and the broader community. Acts of giving in the workplace, such as mentorship, collaboration, and community service initiatives, can enhance job satisfaction and foster a sense of purpose among employees. This, in turn, can lead to increased productivity, creativity, and overall organizational success. The joy that arises from giving in the workplace demonstrates that generosity is not only good for the soul but also good for business.

The joy of giving also has the potential to transcend cultural and geographic boundaries, fostering global solidarity and cooperation. In a world that is increasingly interconnected, acts of giving can build bridges between diverse communities and promote understanding and empathy. International aid and development efforts, for example, are powerful expressions of global altruism, providing support and resources to those in need across the world. These acts of giving create a sense of shared humanity and common purpose, reminding us that we are all part of a global community. The joy that arises from giving on a global scale is a testament to the power of generosity to unite and uplift people from all walks of life.

Moreover, the joy of giving can inspire and drive social change. When individuals and communities come together to address social injustices and support marginalized populations, they create a more equitable and just society. Acts of giving that focus on advocacy, education, and empowerment can lead to systemic changes that benefit everyone. The joy that arises from contributing to social change is a powerful motivator, encouraging individuals to continue their efforts and inspiring others to join the cause. This collective joy of giving has the potential to transform societies, creating a world where everyone has the opportunity to thrive.

The environmental realm is another area where the joy of giving can have a profound impact. Acts of environmental stewardship, such as conservation efforts, sustainable living practices, and advocacy for climate action, demonstrate a deep concern for the well-being of the planet and future generations. These acts of giving not only benefit the environment but also provide a sense of purpose and fulfillment for those involved. The joy that arises from giving to the environment is a reminder that our actions can have far-reaching effects, contributing to the health and sustainability of the planet.

Ultimately, the joy of giving is a reflection of our shared humanity and interconnectedness. It reminds us that we are part of a larger whole and that our actions can have a meaningful impact on the lives of others. The joy that arises from giving is a powerful force that can transform individuals, relationships, communities, and the world. It is a source of hope, resilience, and inspiration, reminding us of the inherent goodness within us all.

By embracing the joy of giving, we open ourselves to a world of possibilities and connections. We discover that true fulfillment comes not from what we receive, but from what we give. The joy of giving teaches us that we have the power to make a difference, to bring light to others' lives, and to create a more compassionate and caring world. It is a testament to the enduring power of love, kindness, and generosity, and a reminder that the greatest joy in life often comes from the simple act of giving.

The joy of giving is a profound and transformative experience that enriches the lives of both the giver and the recipient. It is a source of purpose, fulfillment, and connection, fostering empathy, compassion, and community. The joy that arises from giving is a powerful force that can inspire positive change and create a more caring and supportive world. By embracing the joy of giving, we unlock the potential for personal growth, stronger relationships, and a more just and equitable society. The joy of giving is a reminder of the inherent goodness within us all and the profound impact that our actions can have on the lives of others.

True listening is a sacred act, a gift we offer to others that validates their existence and deepens our own understanding. When we listen with an open heart and mind, we create a space for transformation and connection.

💗💗💗

THREE

BUILDING EMPATHY

Empathy is the cornerstone of meaningful human connections and a critical component of altruism. It involves the ability to understand and share the feelings of others, to see the world from their perspective, and to respond with compassion. Building empathy is a lifelong process that enhances our interactions, deepens our relationships, and fosters a more compassionate and connected society. This essay explores the multifaceted nature of empathy, the importance of developing it, and practical ways to cultivate this vital trait.

At its core, empathy is about tuning into the emotions and experiences of others. It requires active listening, openness, and a genuine interest in understanding another person's inner world. When we empathize, we move beyond our own concerns and immerse ourselves in someone else's reality. This shift from self-focus to other-focus is transformative, enabling us to connect with others on a profound level. Empathy bridges the gap between individuals, creating a sense of shared humanity and mutual understanding.

The ability to empathize is deeply rooted in our biology. Neuroscientific research has identified specific neural circuits, known as mirror neurons, that are activated both when we perform an action and when we observe someone else performing the same action. These neurons play a crucial role in our capacity for empathy, allowing us to mirror and internalize the experiences of others. This biological basis for empathy underscores its fundamental importance to human socialization and cooperation.

Empathy is not a static trait but a dynamic skill that can be developed and strengthened over time. Like any skill, building empathy requires practice, reflection, and a willingness to grow. One of the foundational steps in cultivating empathy is active listening. Active listening involves fully engaging with the speaker, paying close attention to their words, tone, and body language, and responding thoughtfully. It requires setting aside distractions and being present in the moment. Through active listening, we signal to others that their experiences and emotions are valued and understood.

Another essential aspect of building empathy is practicing perspective-taking. Perspective-taking involves imagining oneself in another person's situation, considering their thoughts, feelings, and motivations. This mental exercise helps us appreciate the complexity of their experiences and challenges. It encourages us to move beyond superficial judgments and develop a deeper understanding of their circumstances. By regularly engaging in perspective-taking, we expand our capacity for empathy and become more attuned to the needs and emotions of others.

Empathy also flourishes in an environment of openness and vulnerability. When we share our own feelings and experiences with others, we create a space for reciprocal empathy. Vulnerability fosters trust and intimacy, as it signals a willingness to be seen and understood. By being open about our own struggles and emotions, we invite others to do the same, creating a mutual exchange of empathy. This process not only deepens our connections but also reinforces the importance of empathy in our relationships.

Cultivating empathy requires a commitment to continuous learning and self-awareness. It involves recognizing our own biases and assumptions that may hinder our ability to empathize with others. Reflecting on our interactions and considering how our perspectives and reactions might differ from those of others can help us identify areas for growth. Engaging with diverse perspectives and experiences, through reading, conversations, or exposure to different cultures, broadens our understanding and enhances our ability to empathize.

The practice of mindfulness can also support the development of empathy. Mindfulness involves paying attention to the present moment with a non-judgmental and open attitude. By cultivating mindfulness, we become more aware of our own emotions and reactions, as well as those of others. This heightened awareness enables us to respond with greater empathy and compassion. Mindfulness practices, such as meditation or deep breathing, can help us develop the mental clarity and emotional regulation needed to empathize effectively.

Empathy is not only beneficial for personal relationships but also has profound implications for broader social and societal dynamics. In the context of social justice, empathy is a powerful tool for recognizing and addressing systemic inequalities and injustices. When we empathize with those who have been marginalized or oppressed, we are more likely to advocate for their rights and support efforts to create a more equitable society. Empathy motivates us to take action, to stand in solidarity with others, and to work towards positive change.

In the workplace, empathy is a critical component of effective leadership and teamwork. Leaders who demonstrate empathy are better equipped to understand and address the needs and concerns of their employees. They create a supportive and inclusive work environment where individuals feel valued and heard. Empathetic leaders foster trust and collaboration, which are essential for organizational success. Similarly, team members who empathize with one another are more likely to communicate openly, resolve conflicts constructively, and support each other's growth and development.

Empathy also plays a vital role in education. Teachers who empathize with their students are better able to create a positive and nurturing learning environment. They understand the diverse backgrounds and experiences that students bring to the classroom and tailor their teaching methods to meet individual needs. Empathetic educators build strong relationships with their students, encouraging engagement, motivation, and academic success. Moreover, teaching empathy as a core value helps students develop social and emotional skills that are essential for their personal and professional lives.

Parenting is another domain where empathy is crucial. Parents who empathize with their children provide the emotional support and understanding needed for healthy development. Empathetic parenting involves listening to children, validating their feelings, and guiding them with compassion and patience. This approach fosters secure attachment, resilience, and emotional intelligence in children. By modeling empathy, parents also teach their children how to empathize with others, laying the foundation for strong interpersonal skills and positive relationships.

The impact of empathy extends to global issues, such as humanitarian efforts and international relations. When individuals and nations empathize with those affected by crises, such as natural disasters, conflicts, or poverty, they are more likely to offer aid and support. Empathy drives humanitarian action, from providing immediate relief to addressing long-term needs and rebuilding communities. On a global scale, empathy can foster cooperation and understanding between countries, promoting peace and stability.

Despite its importance, empathy faces challenges in a world characterized by rapid technological advancement and social fragmentation. The rise of digital communication, while offering unprecedented connectivity, can also create barriers to empathy. Online interactions often lack the nuances of face-to-face communication, making it harder to fully understand and connect with others' emotions. Additionally, the anonymity of the internet can sometimes lead to dehumanizing behavior and reduced empathy. To counter these challenges, it is essential to cultivate empathy both online and offline, prioritizing meaningful and respectful interactions.

Another challenge to empathy is the tendency towards empathy fatigue, especially for individuals in caregiving or helping professions. Constant exposure to others' suffering can lead to emotional exhaustion and burnout. To sustain empathy, it is important to practice self-care and set healthy boundaries. This involves recognizing one's own limits, seeking support when needed, and engaging in activities that replenish emotional and mental energy. By taking care of ourselves, we can continue to offer genuine and sustained empathy to others.

Building empathy is not only a personal endeavor but also a collective responsibility. Societies and institutions play a crucial role in fostering empathy through policies, programs, and cultural norms. Educational systems that prioritize social and emotional learning, workplaces that value emotional intelligence, and media that highlight diverse stories and experiences all contribute to a more empathetic world. Community initiatives, such as volunteer programs and social support networks, provide opportunities for individuals to engage in empathetic actions and build connections.

The transformative power of empathy lies in its ability to create a more compassionate and interconnected world. When we empathize with others, we break down barriers and build bridges of understanding and trust. Empathy allows us to see the humanity in each person, to recognize our shared struggles and joys, and to respond with kindness and support. It is a powerful force for good, inspiring us to act with integrity, compassion, and a commitment to the well-being of all.

Ultimately, building empathy is a journey of personal and collective growth. It requires us to look beyond ourselves, to embrace vulnerability, and to engage with the world with an open heart and mind. As we cultivate empathy, we enrich our own lives and contribute to a more just, inclusive, and compassionate society. The journey of building empathy is one of the most meaningful and impactful endeavors we can undertake, as it shapes the quality of our relationships, our communities, and our world. By nurturing empathy within ourselves and others, we create a legacy of kindness and connection that will endure for generations to come.

ᗅᗅᗅ

Volunteering is not just about helping others; it is a journey of self-discovery and personal growth. By offering our time and talents, we discover hidden strengths, broaden our perspectives, and find a deeper sense of purpose.

▷▷▷

FOUR

Everyday Acts of Kindness

Everyday acts of kindness, though often simple and spontaneous, possess a profound capacity to transform lives and foster a sense of community and belonging. These small gestures, which can range from a friendly smile to helping someone carry groceries, create ripples of positivity that extend far beyond the immediate interaction. The cumulative effect of these acts contributes to a more compassionate and connected world, demonstrating that kindness is a powerful force for good.

Kindness begins with awareness and a genuine concern for the well-being of others. It is rooted in empathy, the ability to understand and share the feelings of another person. When we practice kindness, we acknowledge the humanity in others and respond to their needs with compassion and care. This acknowledgment fosters a sense of connection and trust, breaking down barriers and building bridges of understanding.

One of the most beautiful aspects of everyday acts of kindness is their accessibility. Kindness does not require grand gestures or significant resources; it can be practiced by anyone, anywhere, at any time. A simple act like holding the door open for someone, offering a compliment, or lending a helping hand can brighten someone's day and create a moment of connection. These small acts of kindness are often spontaneous and genuine, arising from a moment of empathy and a desire to make someone else's life a little easier.

The impact of these acts extends beyond the immediate recipients. Kindness has a contagious quality; witnessing or experiencing an act of kindness can inspire others to pay it forward. This creates a chain reaction of goodwill, as each act of kindness encourages more acts of kindness. This ripple effect can transform communities, fostering an environment where people look out for one another and support each other's well-being. In this way, everyday acts of kindness contribute to a culture of compassion and mutual respect.

Kindness also has significant benefits for the person performing the act. Engaging in acts of kindness can boost our own mood and sense of well-being. Studies have shown that performing kind acts can reduce stress, increase happiness, and even improve physical health. When we act kindly, our brains release endorphins, which produce feelings of pleasure and satisfaction. This "helper's high" reinforces the behavior, making us more likely to continue performing acts of kindness. Additionally, kindness fosters a sense of purpose and fulfillment, as we see the positive impact of our actions on others.

In personal relationships, everyday acts of kindness are the building blocks of trust and intimacy. Small gestures of care and consideration, such as listening attentively, offering support, or expressing appreciation, strengthen our connections with others. These acts demonstrate that we value and respect the people in our lives, creating a foundation of mutual respect and understanding. Over time, these acts of kindness accumulate, deepening our bonds and enhancing the quality of our relationships. They also help to navigate conflicts and challenges, as kindness and empathy foster a more cooperative and forgiving dynamic.

In the workplace, kindness plays a crucial role in creating a positive and productive environment. Acts of kindness among colleagues, such as offering help with a project, acknowledging someone's hard work, or simply being friendly and approachable, contribute to a supportive and collaborative atmosphere. This not only enhances job satisfaction and morale but also improves teamwork and efficiency. Leaders who model kindness and compassion set a tone of respect and inclusivity, encouraging others to do the same. This fosters a culture where everyone feels valued and motivated to contribute their best.

In educational settings, kindness is essential for creating a safe and nurturing learning environment. Teachers who practice kindness and empathy build strong relationships with their students, fostering trust and engagement. Acts of kindness in the classroom, such as encouraging words, patience, and understanding, support students' emotional and academic growth. When students feel respected and cared for, they are more likely to be motivated and confident in their learning. Additionally, teaching kindness as a core value helps students develop social and emotional skills that are crucial for their success in school and in life. Kindness encourages cooperation, respect for diversity, and conflict resolution skills, creating a more harmonious and inclusive learning environment.

In our increasingly interconnected world, where conflicts and divisions seem to dominate the headlines, everyday acts of kindness serve as a reminder of our shared humanity. They demonstrate that compassion, empathy, and generosity are universal values that transcend cultural, religious, and political boundaries. When we practice kindness, we contribute to a more peaceful and harmonious world, one small act at a time.

The ripple effect of kindness is undeniable. It starts with a single act, a moment of connection between two individuals. This act then inspires others to act kindly, creating a chain reaction of goodwill that spreads throughout communities and even across the globe. The power of kindness lies in its ability to connect us to one another, reminding us that we are all part of something larger than ourselves.

Everyday acts of kindness may seem small and insignificant, but their impact is immeasurable. They foster connection, build trust, and create a more compassionate and harmonious world. Whether in personal relationships, workplaces, or educational settings, kindness plays a crucial role in promoting well-being, productivity, and positive social interactions. Let us all strive to integrate kindness into our daily lives, recognizing that even the smallest gestures can have a profound and lasting impact on ourselves and others.

Giving without expectation is the purest form of altruism, a selfless act that liberates us from the chains of attachment and opens us up to the experience of true abundance. It is a gift that keeps on giving, enriching our lives in countless ways.

ᗐᗐᗐ

FIVE

THE POWER OF LISTENING

In our relentless pursuit of self-expression and the clamor of our own thoughts, we often forget the profound power of listening. It is a transformative act, an alchemical process that can transmute ordinary interactions into extraordinary connections, fostering empathy, understanding, and profound change. True listening goes beyond merely hearing the words spoken; it involves a deep engagement with the speaker, an openness to their experience, and a willingness to receive their message with an open heart and mind.

At its core, listening is an act of generosity. It is a gift we offer to others, a validation of their existence and a recognition of their inherent worth. When we truly listen, we create a safe and supportive space for others to express themselves, to share their stories, and to feel heard and understood. This act of generosity not only benefits the speaker but also enriches our own lives, expanding our perspectives, deepening our empathy, and fostering a sense of interconnectedness.

Listening is an art, a skill that requires patience, presence, and a willingness to set aside our own agendas. It involves quieting the chatter of our minds, suspending judgment, and truly focusing on the person in front of us. It means listening not just to the words spoken but also to the emotions conveyed, the unspoken messages hidden beneath the surface.

True listening is an active process, requiring us to engage all of our senses. It involves paying attention to the speaker's body language, tone of voice, and facial expressions. It means noticing the pauses, the hesitations, and the subtle shifts in energy that reveal the deeper meaning behind their words.

When we listen with our whole being, we create a sacred space where transformation can occur. The speaker feels seen, heard, and valued, which can empower them to explore their own thoughts and feelings more deeply. They may gain new insights, clarify their values, or find the courage to make difficult decisions.

The act of listening also transforms us. By opening ourselves up to the experiences of others, we expand our own understanding of the world. We learn to see things from different perspectives, to challenge our assumptions, and to embrace diversity. We also cultivate empathy and compassion, recognizing that we are all interconnected and that our actions have a ripple effect on others.

The power of listening extends far beyond individual interactions. It can transform communities, heal relationships, and even bridge divides between cultures and nations. When we listen to those who are different from us, we break down barriers of prejudice and misunderstanding. We create opportunities for dialogue, collaboration, and mutual respect.

In a world that is often characterized by conflict and division, listening offers a powerful antidote. It reminds us of our shared humanity, our common struggles, and our collective aspirations. It creates a space for healing, reconciliation, and the possibility of a more just and equitable world.

The power of listening is not limited to the realm of interpersonal relationships. It also applies to our relationship with ourselves. By listening to our own inner voice, our intuition, we can gain valuable insights into our needs, desires, and motivations. We can also access a deeper level of self-awareness, which can help us to make more authentic and aligned choices in life.

Practicing listening is a lifelong journey, one that requires us to continually challenge ourselves to be more present, more open, and more compassionate. It involves cultivating a genuine curiosity about others, a willingness to learn from their experiences, and a desire to connect on a deeper level.

By embracing the power of listening, we can transform not only our own lives but also the lives of those around us. We can create a ripple effect of compassion, understanding, and connection that extends far beyond our individual interactions.

ppp

Knowledge is a beacon of light, illuminating the path towards a brighter future. When we share our knowledge with others, we empower them to reach their full potential and create positive change in the world.

▷▷▷

SIX

Volunteering: Time Well Spent

The act of volunteering, the selfless offering of one's time and energy to a cause greater than oneself, is an alchemical process that transforms not only the lives of those we serve but also our own hearts and souls. It is a gift we give freely, a gesture of compassion and solidarity that transcends boundaries of class, race, and creed. Volunteering is not merely a pastime or a charitable act; it is an investment in our shared humanity, a testament to our interconnectedness, and a pathway to personal growth and fulfillment.

Volunteering can take many forms, from serving meals at a homeless shelter to tutoring underprivileged children to advocating for environmental protection. It can be a one-time commitment or a lifelong passion. Regardless of the form it takes, volunteering offers a multitude of benefits, both for the recipients of our service and for ourselves.

For those we serve, volunteering can be a lifeline, a source of hope and support in times of need. It can provide essential services, such as food, shelter, and medical care, to those who are struggling to make ends meet. It can also offer emotional support, companionship, and a sense of belonging to those who are isolated or marginalized. By volunteering our time and skills, we empower others, giving them the tools and resources they need to overcome challenges and create a better future for themselves.

However, the benefits of volunteering are not limited to those we serve. Volunteering is a transformative experience that can enrich our own lives in countless ways. It can broaden our perspectives, challenge our assumptions, and deepen our empathy for others. It can also boost our self-esteem, enhance our social connections, and give us a sense of purpose and meaning.

When we volunteer, we step outside of our comfort zones and engage with people from different backgrounds and walks of life. This exposure to diversity can challenge our preconceived notions, expand our worldview, and foster a greater appreciation for the richness of human experience. We learn to see the world through the eyes of others, to understand their struggles, and to celebrate their triumphs.

Volunteering can also connect us to a community of like-minded individuals who share our passion for service. These connections can provide us with a sense of belonging, support, and inspiration. We can learn from each other's experiences, share our challenges and successes, and build lasting friendships that enrich our lives.

Furthermore, volunteering can be a powerful antidote to the stresses and anxieties of modern life. When we focus our attention on helping others, we shift our focus away from our own problems and concerns. This can reduce stress, boost our mood, and improve our overall well-being. Studies have shown that volunteering can lower blood pressure, strengthen the immune system, and even increase longevity.

The act of giving, in and of itself, is a rewarding experience. When we volunteer our time and energy, we tap into our innate capacity for compassion and generosity. This can lead to a sense of purpose, fulfillment, and joy. We discover that giving is not a sacrifice, but a gift we give to ourselves as well as to others.

Volunteering is not just about doing good deeds; it is about cultivating a spirit of generosity and service that can transform our lives and the world around us. It is about recognizing our interconnectedness and embracing our responsibility to care for one another.

In a world that often seems focused on individual achievement and material gain, volunteering offers a powerful counter-narrative. It reminds us that true wealth lies not in what we accumulate but in what we give away. It teaches us that the greatest joy comes not from pursuing our own self-interest but from serving a cause greater than ourselves.

ppp

Generosity in action is the embodiment of compassion, a tangible expression of our interconnectedness. Every act of kindness, no matter how small, has the power to transform lives and uplift communities.

ᗽᗽᗽ

SEVEN

GIVING WITHOUT EXPECTATION

The act of giving, when done with a pure heart and without the expectation of reciprocity, is an act of profound transformation. It is a form of alchemy that transmutes not only the lives of those who receive but also the very essence of the giver. In this selfless act, we tap into the wellspring of compassion that resides within us, unlocking a reservoir of joy, peace, and interconnectedness. Giving without expectation is not merely a charitable act; it is a spiritual practice, a way of life that enriches our souls and elevates our consciousness.

In a world often driven by self-interest and material gain, the concept of giving without expectation may seem counterintuitive. We are conditioned to believe that our actions should be motivated by a desire for reward or recognition. However, true giving transcends these ego-driven impulses, flowing from a place of genuine compassion and a desire to alleviate suffering.

When we give without expectation, we liberate ourselves from the shackles of attachment and the burden of reciprocity. We give simply because it feels right, because it aligns with our values, and because we recognize the inherent dignity and worth of every human being. This act of selfless giving creates a ripple effect of positivity, spreading joy and compassion throughout the world.

The benefits of giving without expectation are numerous and profound. For the recipient, it can be a lifeline, a source of hope and inspiration in times of need. It can provide essential resources, such as food, shelter, and medical care, or it can offer emotional support, encouragement, and a sense of belonging. When we give without expectation, we empower others, allowing them to rise above their circumstances and create a better future for themselves.

However, the benefits of giving without expectation are not limited to those who receive. The act of giving itself is a transformative experience that can enrich our own lives in countless ways. It can deepen our empathy, expand our compassion, and foster a sense of interconnectedness with all beings.

When we give without expectation, we open ourselves up to the experience of abundance. We realize that the more we give, the more we receive, not in material terms, but in spiritual and emotional riches. We experience a sense of joy, peace, and fulfillment that comes from knowing that we have made a positive difference in the world.

Furthermore, giving without expectation can be a powerful antidote to the stresses and anxieties of modern life. When we focus our attention on helping others, we shift our focus away from our own problems and concerns. This can reduce stress, boost our mood, and improve our overall well-being. Studies have shown that altruistic behavior can lower blood pressure, strengthen the immune system, and even increase longevity.

The act of giving without expectation also fosters a sense of gratitude and appreciation. When we recognize the abundance in our own lives and the opportunity to share it with others, we cultivate a deep sense of gratitude for all that we have been given. This gratitude, in turn, can lead to greater happiness, resilience, and a more positive outlook on life.

Giving without expectation is not always easy. It requires us to let go of our ego-driven desires for recognition and reward. It challenges us to step outside of our comfort zones and embrace the vulnerability of selfless service. However, the rewards of this practice are immeasurable.

By embracing the practice of giving without expectation, we can transform our lives and the world around us. We can create a ripple effect of kindness, compassion, and generosity that can touch the lives of countless individuals. We can also discover a deeper sense of meaning, purpose, and fulfillment in our own lives, knowing that we are contributing to a more just, equitable, and compassionate world.

Furthermore, giving without expectation can be a powerful antidote to the stresses and anxieties of modern life. When we focus our attention on helping others, we shift our focus away from our own problems and concerns. This can reduce stress, boost our mood, and improve our overall well-being. Studies have shown that altruistic behavior can lower blood pressure, strengthen the immune system, and even increase longevity.

The act of giving without expectation also fosters a sense of gratitude and appreciation. When we recognize the abundance in our own lives and the opportunity to share it with others, we cultivate a deep sense of gratitude for all that we have been given. This gratitude, in turn, can lead to greater happiness, resilience, and a more positive outlook on life.

Giving without expectation is not always easy. It requires us to let go of our ego-driven desires for recognition and reward. It challenges us to step outside of our comfort zones and embrace the vulnerability of selfless service. However, the rewards of this practice are immeasurable.

By embracing the practice of giving without expectation, we can transform our lives and the world around us. We can create a ripple effect of kindness, compassion, and generosity that can touch the lives of countless individuals. We can also discover a deeper sense of meaning, purpose, and fulfillment in our own lives, knowing that we are contributing to a more just, equitable, and compassionate world.

It is important to note that giving without expectation does not mean giving indiscriminately or without boundaries. It is essential to discern where our energy is best directed and to ensure that our giving is sustainable and does not lead to burnout. It is also important to recognize that not everyone may be ready or willing to receive our gifts, and that is okay. The act of giving is a gift in itself, regardless of the outcome.

In the end, giving without expectation is a choice, a conscious decision to live a life of generosity, compassion, and service. It is a way of aligning our actions with our deepest values and creating a world that is more loving, just, and equitable for all.

ᗞᗞᗞ

A giving mindset is a choice, a conscious decision to prioritize the well-being of others and to create a more equitable and harmonious world. It is a mindset that fosters abundance, joy, and fulfillment in our own lives.

♥♥♥

EIGHT

THE GIFT OF KNOWLEDGE

In the vast tapestry of human existence, knowledge stands as a beacon of illumination, guiding us through the labyrinth of ignorance and empowering us to shape our destinies. The gift of knowledge, however, is not merely an accumulation of facts and figures; it is a dynamic force that transcends the boundaries of information, encompassing wisdom, understanding, and the ability to apply what we learn to create positive change in our lives and the world around us.

Knowledge, in its essence, is the awareness and understanding of facts, truths, or principles. It is the information we gather through learning, observation, and experience. It is the foundation upon which we build our understanding of the world and ourselves. Knowledge empowers us to make informed decisions, solve problems, and navigate the complexities of life.

However, knowledge is not simply about acquiring information; it is about transforming that information into wisdom. Wisdom is the ability to apply knowledge to real-life situations, to discern what is important, and to make sound judgments. It is the synthesis of knowledge and experience, a deeper understanding that comes from reflection, introspection, and a willingness to learn from our mistakes.

The gift of knowledge is not bestowed upon a select few; it is a universal inheritance, available to all who seek it. It is not limited to formal education or academic institutions; it can be found in the pages of books, the stories of our elders, the lessons of nature, and the experiences of our daily lives.

Knowledge is a gift that keeps on giving. The more we learn, the more we realize how much more there is to know. This realization can be both humbling and exhilarating. It reminds us that we are part of a vast and interconnected universe, and that our individual knowledge is but a small drop in the ocean of collective wisdom.

The pursuit of knowledge is a lifelong journey, one that requires curiosity, open-mindedness, and a willingness to challenge our assumptions. It is not about memorizing facts or regurgitating information, but about actively engaging with ideas, exploring different perspectives, and seeking to understand the underlying principles that govern the world.

When we approach knowledge with a spirit of curiosity and open-mindedness, we open ourselves up to a world of possibilities. We discover new ideas, new ways of thinking, and new ways of being. We challenge our preconceived notions, expand our worldview, and deepen our understanding of ourselves and others.

Knowledge is not just about intellectual growth; it is also about personal transformation. As we learn and grow, we become more self-aware, more compassionate, and more connected to the world around us. We develop a deeper appreciation for the diversity of human experience, and we gain a greater understanding of our place in the universe.

The gift of knowledge is not meant to be hoarded; it is meant to be shared. When we share our knowledge with others, we not only empower them, but we also strengthen our own understanding. The act of teaching can be a powerful learning experience, as it forces us to clarify our own thinking and to communicate complex ideas in a clear and concise way.

Furthermore, sharing our knowledge can create a ripple effect of positive change. By educating others, we empower them to make informed decisions, solve problems, and create a better future for themselves and their communities. We also contribute to the collective wisdom of humanity, adding our own unique insights and perspectives to the ever-growing tapestry of human knowledge.

The gift of knowledge is a precious treasure, one that we should cherish and nurture. It is a key that unlocks the door to a world of possibilities, a compass that guides us on our journey of self-discovery, and a light that illuminates the path towards a brighter future. By embracing the gift of knowledge, we can transform our lives, our communities, and the world around us.

ᗞᗞᗞ

Gratitude is the key to unlocking the abundance that surrounds us. By appreciating the blessings in our lives, we cultivate a sense of joy, peace, and contentment that radiates outward and inspires others.

ᗥᗥᗥ

NINE

GENEROSITY IN ACTION

Generosity in action is the embodiment of compassion, a tangible manifestation of our interconnectedness, and a testament to the inherent goodness of the human spirit. It is a force that transcends boundaries, unites communities, and creates a ripple effect of positive change that can transform lives and uplift entire societies. Generosity in action is not merely about donating money or resources; it encompasses a wide range of behaviors, from small acts of kindness to grand philanthropic endeavors. It is a way of being, a mindset that prioritizes the well-being of others and seeks to create a more just, equitable, and compassionate world.

At its core, generosity in action is driven by empathy, the ability to understand and share the feelings of others. When we see someone in need, whether it be a neighbor struggling to make ends meet, a community devastated by natural disaster, or a global crisis affecting millions, our empathy motivates us to take action. We recognize that we are all part of a larger human family, and that our actions have a ripple effect on the lives of others.

Generosity in action can take many forms. It can be as simple as offering a helping hand to a stranger, volunteering our time and skills to a local organization, or donating money to a worthy cause. It can also involve advocating for social justice, supporting environmental protection, or promoting education and opportunity for all.

The impact of generosity in action is far-reaching. It can provide essential resources and support to those in need, empowering them to overcome challenges and create a better future for themselves. It can also inspire others to act, creating a chain reaction of goodwill that spreads throughout communities and across the globe.

When we witness acts of generosity, we are reminded of the inherent goodness of humanity. We see that even in the face of adversity, there are people who are willing to step up and help others, without expecting anything in return. This can restore our faith in humanity and inspire us to be more generous in our own lives.

Generosity in action is not just about giving to others; it is also about receiving. When we give generously, we open ourselves up to the experience of abundance. We realize that the more we give, the more we receive, not in material terms, but in spiritual and emotional riches. We experience a sense of joy, fulfillment, and gratitude that comes from knowing that we have made a positive difference in the world.

Furthermore, generosity in action can be a powerful antidote to the stresses and anxieties of modern life. When we focus our attention on helping others, we shift our focus away from our own problems and concerns. This can reduce stress, boost our mood, and improve our overall well-being. Studies have shown that altruistic behavior can lower blood pressure, strengthen the immune system, and even increase longevity.

The act of giving also fosters a sense of connection and belonging.

When we work together with others towards a common goal, we build relationships, strengthen communities, and create a sense of shared purpose. This sense of connection can be a powerful source of support and resilience in times of adversity.

Generosity in action is not a one-time event; it is a way of life. It is a commitment to living with an open heart, a generous spirit, and a willingness to take action to make the world a better place. It is a recognition that our actions, no matter how small, can have a profound and lasting impact on the lives of others.

In a world that often seems focused on individual achievement and material gain, generosity in action offers a different path. It is a path that leads to greater happiness, fulfillment, and connection. It is a path that reminds us of our shared humanity and our responsibility to care for one another. By embracing generosity in action, we can create a world that is more just, equitable, and compassionate for all.

ﭏﭏﭏ

Community building through giving is a powerful force for positive change. When we come together to share our resources, skills, and time, we create a vibrant and supportive environment where everyone can thrive.

❦❦❦

TEN

CULTIVATING A GIVING MINDSET

Cultivating a giving mindset is a transformative journey, an inner alchemy that shifts our focus from self-interest to compassion, abundance to generosity, and isolation to interconnectedness. It is a conscious choice to embrace a way of being that prioritizes the well-being of others and seeks to create a more equitable and harmonious world. This mindset is not simply about donating money or resources; it is a deep-rooted belief in the power of giving to uplift both the giver and the receiver, a recognition that our actions, no matter how small, can create a ripple effect of positive change.

At its core, a giving mindset is rooted in empathy and compassion. It is the ability to step outside of our own perspectives and experiences and truly understand the feelings and needs of others. When we cultivate empathy, we develop a deeper sense of connection to the world around us, recognizing that we are all part of a larger human family. This interconnectedness fuels our desire to contribute to the well-being of others, to share our resources, and to alleviate suffering wherever we encounter it.

Cultivating a giving mindset is not a matter of simply changing our behavior; it requires a fundamental shift in our beliefs and values. It involves recognizing that true abundance lies not in what we accumulate but in what we share. It means embracing the idea that giving is not a sacrifice but an investment in our own happiness and well-being.

This shift in perspective can be challenging, as we are often bombarded with messages that equate success with material wealth and personal achievement. However, by consciously choosing to focus on giving, we can break free from these limiting beliefs and discover a deeper sense of purpose and fulfillment.

There are many ways to cultivate a giving mindset. One approach is to start small, by incorporating acts of kindness into our daily lives. This might involve holding the door open for someone, offering a compliment, or volunteering our time to a local organization. These small acts of generosity not only benefit others but also create a positive feedback loop, reinforcing our own sense of compassion and generosity.

Another way to cultivate a giving mindset is to practice gratitude. When we take the time to appreciate the abundance in our own lives, we are more likely to feel a sense of generosity towards others. Gratitude can be cultivated through simple practices such as keeping a gratitude journal, expressing appreciation to loved ones, or taking time to savor the simple joys of life.

Giving can also be cultivated through mindfulness practices, such as meditation and yoga. These practices help us to quiet our minds, connect with our hearts, and cultivate a greater sense of compassion and empathy. By cultivating mindfulness, we become more aware of the needs of others and more attuned to the ways in which we can contribute to their well-being.

As we cultivate a giving mindset, we may find that our capacity for generosity expands beyond our expectations. We may discover new ways to give, new causes to support, and new opportunities to make a positive difference in the world. We may also find that our own lives are enriched in unexpected ways, as we experience the joy, fulfillment, and connection that come from living a life of service.

The journey of cultivating a giving mindset is a lifelong process, one that requires ongoing commitment and self-reflection. It is not always easy, as we may encounter challenges, setbacks, and moments of doubt. However, the rewards of this journey are immeasurable. By embracing a giving mindset, we not only transform our own lives but also contribute to the creation of a more compassionate, equitable, and sustainable world for all.

የየየ

Giving as a family is a legacy of love, a tradition that instills values of compassion, generosity, and empathy in future generations. It is a gift that strengthens family bonds and creates lasting memories.

♡♡♡

ELEVEN

THE ROLE OF GRATITUDE

Gratitude, the simple act of acknowledging and appreciating the good things in our lives, is a profound force that can transform our hearts, minds, and spirits. It is not merely a fleeting emotion or a polite gesture; it is a way of being, a mindset that shifts our focus from scarcity to abundance, from lack to fulfillment. When we cultivate gratitude, we open ourselves up to the richness of life, recognizing the blessings that surround us and appreciating the beauty, kindness, and generosity that exist in the world.

At its core, gratitude is a recognition of the interconnectedness of all things. It is an acknowledgment that we are not solely responsible for our successes and that we are supported by a vast network of people, circumstances, and forces beyond our control. When we express gratitude, we acknowledge the contributions of others, the gifts of nature, and the blessings of life itself. This recognition fosters a sense of humility, connection, and appreciation, allowing us to see the world through a lens of abundance rather than scarcity.

The practice of gratitude has a profound impact on our well-being. Studies have shown that individuals who regularly practice gratitude experience a wide range of benefits, including increased happiness, resilience, optimism, and life satisfaction. They also tend to have stronger relationships, better physical health, and improved sleep quality. Gratitude has even been shown to reduce symptoms of depression and anxiety, and to increase self-esteem and self-worth.

One of the most powerful aspects of gratitude is its ability to shift our focus from what we lack to what we have. When we take the time to acknowledge and appreciate the good things in our lives, we naturally begin to feel more content and fulfilled. We become less preoccupied with our perceived shortcomings and more appreciative of the blessings that surround us. This shift in perspective can lead to greater happiness, peace of mind, and a more positive outlook on life.

Gratitude also has a ripple effect, spreading positivity and goodwill to those around us. When we express gratitude to others, we not only uplift their spirits but also inspire them to be more grateful themselves. This creates a virtuous cycle of appreciation and kindness, strengthening our relationships and fostering a more supportive and compassionate community.

The practice of gratitude can take many forms. It can be as simple as taking a few moments each day to reflect on the things we are grateful for, or it can involve more structured practices such as keeping a gratitude journal, writing thank-you notes, or performing acts of kindness. The key is to find a practice that resonates with you and to incorporate it into your daily routine.

As we cultivate gratitude, we may discover that it becomes a natural and spontaneous response to life's experiences. We may find ourselves appreciating the beauty of a sunrise, the kindness of a stranger, or the simple pleasures of a good meal. This heightened awareness of the good things in our lives can lead to a deeper sense of joy, peace, and connection to the world around us.

Gratitude is not just about feeling good; it is also about doing good. When we are grateful, we are more likely to be generous, compassionate, and helpful to others. We are more likely to volunteer our time, donate to charity, and offer support to those in need. This altruistic behavior not only benefits others but also reinforces our own sense of gratitude, creating a positive feedback loop that enhances our well-being.

In the tapestry of life, gratitude is the golden thread that weaves together our experiences, relationships, and aspirations. It is a transformative force that can uplift our spirits, deepen our connections, and empower us to create a more joyful, meaningful, and compassionate world.

ppp

Sustainable giving is about creating lasting change, not just providing temporary relief. It is a commitment to investing in solutions that address the root causes of social and environmental challenges.

♡♡♡

TWELVE
COMMUNITY BUILDING THROUGH GIVING

Community building through giving is an age-old practice, deeply ingrained in the human spirit and essential for the flourishing of societies. It is a transformative process that goes beyond the mere act of donating resources or volunteering time. It involves creating a sense of shared purpose, fostering connections, and empowering individuals to contribute to the collective well-being. When giving is woven into the fabric of a community, it becomes a powerful force for positive change, creating a ripple effect that strengthens social bonds, fosters resilience, and promotes a sense of belonging.

Giving, in its essence, is an act of generosity that transcends the transactional nature of exchange. It is the voluntary offering of resources, time, or expertise to benefit others or a cause without expecting anything in return. Giving can take many forms, from donating money to charity, volunteering at a local soup kitchen, or simply offering a helping hand to a neighbor in need.

When giving is embedded within a community, it creates a culture of reciprocity and mutual support. It encourages individuals to look beyond their own self-interest and contribute to the well-being of others. This, in turn, fosters a sense of shared responsibility and a belief that everyone has a role to play in building a stronger, more vibrant community.

Community building through giving can manifest in various ways. It can involve establishing formal organizations and institutions that provide essential services and support to community members. These organizations might include food banks, shelters, community centers, and educational programs. They provide a platform for individuals to come together, pool their resources, and work towards a common goal.

Giving can also be expressed through informal networks of support, such as neighborhood watch groups, mutual aid societies, and volunteer-led initiatives. These networks foster a sense of connection and belonging among community members, providing them with a safety net and a platform for collective action.

One of the most powerful aspects of community building through giving is its ability to empower individuals. When people are given the opportunity to contribute their time, skills, and resources to a cause they believe in, they feel a sense of agency and purpose. They become active participants in shaping their community, rather than passive recipients of aid. This sense of empowerment can lead to increased self-esteem, confidence, and a greater sense of belonging.

Giving can also bridge divides and foster understanding between different groups within a community. When people from diverse backgrounds come together to volunteer or donate to a shared cause, they have the opportunity to interact with each other, learn from each other, and build relationships based on mutual respect and cooperation. This can break down stereotypes, reduce prejudice, and promote a more inclusive and harmonious community.

Furthermore, community building through giving can be a powerful tool for addressing social challenges and promoting positive change. When individuals come together to tackle issues such as poverty, homelessness, or environmental degradation, they can leverage their collective resources and expertise to create innovative solutions and drive systemic change.

However, it is important to recognize that community building through giving is not a panacea for all social ills. It cannot replace the need for systemic change and government intervention. However, it can complement and enhance these efforts by fostering a sense of shared responsibility and empowering individuals to take action in their own communities.

The practice of giving is not without its challenges. It requires us to confront our own biases, prejudices, and limitations. It challenges us to step outside of our comfort zones and engage with people who may be different from us. It also requires us to grapple with complex issues such as power dynamics, equity, and accountability.

However, the rewards of community building through giving are immeasurable. It can create a more just, equitable, and compassionate world. It can empower individuals, strengthen communities, and foster a sense of shared purpose and belonging.

ppp

Corporate social responsibility is a recognition that businesses have a responsibility to contribute to the well-being of their communities and the planet. By aligning profit with purpose, businesses can create a positive impact that benefits both society and the environment.

❧❧❧

THIRTEEN

GIVING AS A FAMILY

In a world often focused on individual pursuits and material gain, giving as a family emerges as a beacon of hope, illuminating the path towards a more compassionate, connected, and purposeful life. When families come together to share their time, resources, and talents with others, they not only create a positive impact on their communities but also strengthen their own bonds and cultivate a shared sense of values. Giving as a family is not merely a charitable act; it is a transformative experience that enriches the lives of all involved, fostering empathy, compassion, and a deeper understanding of the world around them.

At its core, giving as a family is about creating a shared experience that transcends individual interests and priorities. It is about coming together to support a cause larger than oneself, recognizing that our collective efforts can make a meaningful difference in the lives of others. Whether it's volunteering at a local soup kitchen, donating to a favorite charity, or simply performing acts of kindness in our daily lives, giving as a family creates opportunities for connection, shared learning, and personal growth.

One of the most significant benefits of giving as a family is the opportunity for children to learn and internalize values such as empathy, compassion, and generosity. When children see their parents or caregivers actively involved in helping others, they learn that kindness and generosity are not just abstract concepts, but tangible actions that have a real impact on the world. They learn to see beyond their own needs and desires and to consider the needs of others.

Giving as a family also creates opportunities for shared learning and exploration. Families can research and discuss different causes, volunteer opportunities, and charitable organizations together, learning about the challenges facing their communities and the world at large. This shared learning experience can spark conversations, encourage critical thinking, and foster a deeper understanding of social issues.

Furthermore, giving as a family can strengthen family bonds and create lasting memories. When family members work together towards a common goal, they develop a sense of shared purpose and accomplishment. They learn to rely on each other, communicate effectively, and appreciate each other's strengths and weaknesses. These shared experiences can create lasting bonds of love, trust, and mutual respect.

Giving as a family can also be a fun and rewarding experience. It can create opportunities for bonding, laughter, and shared joy. Whether it's volunteering at a local animal shelter, participating in a community clean-up, or simply baking cookies for a neighbor, giving as a family can be a source of enjoyment and fulfillment for all involved.

The impact of family giving extends beyond the individual family unit. It can create a ripple effect of positivity throughout the community, inspiring others to follow suit and contributing to a more compassionate and connected society. When families give together, they become role models for others, demonstrating the power of collective action and the importance of giving back.

Giving as a family is not just about financial contributions; it can also involve donating time, skills, and expertise. Families can volunteer their time at local organizations, mentor young people, or share their knowledge and expertise with others. These contributions can be just as valuable as financial donations, and they often create deeper and more meaningful connections with the community.

While giving as a family offers numerous benefits, it is important to approach it with intention and purpose. It is essential to choose causes that align with the family's values and interests, and to ensure that everyone in the family feels involved and empowered. It is also important to be mindful of the needs of the community and to ensure that our giving is truly making a positive difference.

In the tapestry of family life, giving is a golden thread that weaves together love, compassion, and shared purpose. It is a gift that keeps on giving, enriching the lives of both the giver and the receiver. By embracing giving as a family, we create a legacy of generosity, compassion, and service that will last for generations to come.

Giving as a family is not just about doing good deeds; it is also about having fun and enjoying each other's company. It can be a source of joy and laughter, as family members bond over shared experiences and create lasting memories. Whether it's volunteering at a local animal shelter, participating in a community clean-up, or simply baking cookies for a neighbor, giving as a family can be a fun and rewarding experience for all involved.

The impact of family giving goes beyond the individual family unit. It ripples throughout the community, inspiring others to follow suit and contributing to a more compassionate and connected society. When families give together, they become role models for others, demonstrating the power of collective action and the importance of giving back. This can create a ripple effect of generosity and goodwill, inspiring others to get involved and make a difference in their own communities.

Giving as a family is not just about financial contributions; it can also involve donating time, skills, and expertise. Families can volunteer their time at local organizations, mentor young people, or share their knowledge and expertise with others. These contributions can be just as valuable as financial donations, and they often create deeper and more meaningful connections with the community.

While giving as a family offers numerous benefits, it is essential to approach it with intention and purpose. It is important to choose causes that align with the family's values and interests, and to ensure that everyone in the family feels involved and empowered. It is also important to be mindful of the needs of the community and to ensure that our giving is truly making a positive difference.

In the tapestry of family life, giving is a golden thread that weaves together love, compassion, and shared purpose. It is a gift that keeps on giving, enriching the lives of both the giver and the receiver. By embracing giving as a family, we create a legacy of generosity, compassion, and service that will last for generations to come.

 PPP

The future of giving is bright, with technology, collaboration, and a growing awareness of interconnectedness transforming the landscape of philanthropy and social impact. It is a future where everyone can contribute to creating a more just, equitable, and sustainable world.

ppp

FOURTEEN

OVERCOMING OBSTACLES TO GIVING

The path of generosity, while profoundly rewarding, is not without its challenges. Numerous obstacles, both internal and external, can hinder our ability to give freely and fully. These barriers can range from financial limitations and time constraints to psychological hurdles such as fear, guilt, and a scarcity mindset. However, by recognizing and addressing these obstacles, we can unlock our capacity for generosity and experience the transformative power of giving.

Financial limitations are often cited as a major obstacle to giving. In a world where resources are finite and economic disparities abound, many individuals may feel that they simply do not have enough to give. However, generosity is not solely measured by monetary contributions. It can manifest in various forms, such as volunteering time, offering skills and expertise, or simply showing kindness and compassion to others. Even small acts of generosity can have a significant impact, both on the recipients and on ourselves. By shifting our focus from the quantity of our giving to the quality of our intention, we can overcome financial limitations and find meaningful ways to contribute.

Time constraints are another common barrier to giving. In our fast-paced, over-scheduled lives, it can be difficult to carve out time for volunteering, donating, or simply engaging in acts of kindness. However, by prioritizing giving and integrating it into our daily routines, we can find creative ways to make a difference, even with limited time. This might involve setting aside a few hours each month for volunteer work, making small donations online, or simply incorporating acts of kindness into our daily interactions with others.

Psychological obstacles can be even more challenging to overcome. Fear, guilt, and a scarcity mindset can all hinder our ability to give freely. Fear of not having enough, fear of being taken advantage of, or fear of judgment from others can all hold us back from expressing our generosity. Guilt, on the other hand, can arise from a sense of not doing enough or not being worthy of giving.

To overcome these psychological barriers, it is essential to cultivate self-compassion and recognize that our capacity for giving is not limited by our perceived flaws or shortcomings. We can also challenge our limiting beliefs by reframing our understanding of abundance. True abundance is not about accumulating material wealth; it is about recognizing the richness of our lives and the interconnectedness of all beings. By shifting our focus from scarcity to abundance, we can unlock our generosity and experience the joy of giving.

Social and cultural norms can also create obstacles to giving. In some cultures, giving is seen as a sign of weakness or a burden on the receiver. In other cultures, there may be a stigma attached to certain types of giving, such as donating to organizations that support marginalized groups. To overcome these social and cultural barriers, it is important to educate ourselves and others about the value of giving, to challenge harmful stereotypes, and to create a culture of generosity and compassion.

Furthermore, it is important to recognize that giving is not a one-size-fits-all proposition. Different individuals have different capacities and preferences for giving. Some may prefer to donate money, while others may prefer to volunteer their time or skills. Some may be drawn to local causes, while others may be more passionate about global issues. The key is to find a way of giving that aligns with our values, interests, and resources.

By recognizing and addressing the various obstacles to giving, we can unlock our innate capacity for generosity and experience the transformative power of this simple act. We can discover that giving is not a burden, but a blessing. It is a way of connecting with others, creating positive change, and enriching our own lives in the process.

ᖃᖃᖃ

*The act of giving is a transformative journey, a
path that leads us to greater self-awareness,
compassion, and connection to the world around us.
It is a journey that reveals the inherent goodness of
the human spirit and our infinite potential for
positive change.*

❦❦❦

FIFTEEN

SUSTAINABLE GIVING

Sustainable giving is a philosophy and practice that recognizes the importance of balancing generosity with longevity, ensuring that our acts of kindness have a lasting impact on both the recipients and ourselves. It's a mindful approach that goes beyond impulsive acts of charity, focusing on creating systems and structures that support ongoing generosity while avoiding burnout and depletion. Sustainable giving acknowledges that true altruism isn't about sporadic bursts of effort, but rather a consistent commitment to making a positive difference in the world.

At its core, sustainable giving involves a shift in perspective from short-term relief to long-term empowerment. Instead of merely addressing immediate needs, it seeks to create sustainable solutions that address the root causes of social and environmental challenges. This might involve supporting education initiatives, investing in community development projects, or advocating for systemic change.

Sustainable giving also recognizes the importance of self-care for those who give. It acknowledges that burnout is a real risk for individuals who dedicate their time and resources to helping others.

By prioritizing self-care, setting boundaries, and practicing mindfulness, givers can ensure that their generosity is sustainable in the long run. This might involve taking breaks, engaging in activities that replenish their energy, and seeking support from others when needed.

Financial sustainability is a crucial aspect of sustainable giving. It involves creating a budget for charitable donations and ensuring that our giving aligns with our financial goals. This might involve setting aside a certain percentage of our income for charitable donations, creating a donor-advised fund, or investing in socially responsible companies. By planning our giving strategically, we can ensure that our generosity is both impactful and sustainable over time.

In addition to financial donations, sustainable giving can also involve sharing our time, skills, and expertise. Volunteering our time to a cause we care about can be a deeply rewarding experience, allowing us to connect with others, make a tangible difference, and gain new skills and perspectives. Offering our expertise as mentors, advisors, or consultants can also provide valuable support to organizations and individuals working towards positive change.

Sustainable giving is not just about individual action; it is also about collective impact. By joining forces with others, we can amplify our efforts and create a greater impact than we could alone. This might involve joining a giving circle, volunteering with a group of friends or colleagues, or partnering with organizations that share our values and goals.

Building a sustainable giving practice requires a long-term commitment and a willingness to adapt and evolve. It is not a one-size-fits-all approach, but rather a personal journey that is unique to each individual. Some people may find that their giving evolves over time, as their interests and priorities change. Others may find that their giving becomes more focused and strategic, as they gain experience and knowledge.

The key is to approach giving with an open mind, a willingness to learn, and a commitment to making a positive impact on the world. By embracing sustainable giving practices, we can ensure that our generosity is not only impactful but also sustainable, creating a legacy of positive change that extends far beyond our own lifetimes.

Sustainable giving is not just a trend or a buzzword; it is a fundamental shift in how we approach philanthropy and social impact. It is a recognition that true generosity is not about short-term fixes but about creating lasting change. By embracing sustainable giving, we can create a world that is more just, equitable, and sustainable for all.

❧❧❧

Let us remember that every act of kindness, no matter how small, can create a ripple effect that extends far beyond our individual lives. By embracing the spirit of giving, we can create a world that is more compassionate, just, and equitable for all.

ᗞᗞᗞ

SIXTEEN

CORPORATE SOCIAL RESPONSIBILITY

Corporate Social Responsibility (CSR) has emerged as a vital component of modern business practice, transcending the traditional profit-driven model and embracing a broader commitment to society and the environment. It is a recognition that businesses have a responsibility to contribute to the well-being of their communities and the planet, not just through their products and services, but also through their actions and impact. CSR is a multi-faceted concept that encompasses a wide range of initiatives, from environmental sustainability and ethical labor practices to philanthropic giving and community engagement. By integrating CSR into their core values and operations, businesses can not only improve their reputation and bottom line but also contribute to a more sustainable and equitable future.

At its heart, CSR is about accountability and transparency. It is about recognizing that businesses do not operate in a vacuum but are part of a complex ecosystem of stakeholders, including employees, customers, suppliers, communities, and the environment. CSR involves taking responsibility for the impact of business activities on these stakeholders and taking proactive steps to mitigate any negative effects. This might involve reducing carbon emissions, implementing fair labor practices, sourcing sustainable materials, or supporting community initiatives.

CSR is not merely a matter of compliance with laws and regulations; it is a commitment to going above and beyond what is legally required. It is about striving to make a positive impact on society and the environment, even when it is not mandated or financially incentivized. This commitment to ethical and responsible behavior can create a virtuous cycle, as it fosters trust and loyalty among stakeholders, leading to increased brand value, customer satisfaction, and employee engagement.

One of the key drivers of CSR is the growing awareness of the social and environmental challenges facing our planet. Climate change, poverty, inequality, and resource depletion are just a few of the pressing issues that demand urgent action. Businesses have a unique opportunity to leverage their resources, expertise, and influence to address these challenges and contribute to a more sustainable future. By integrating CSR into their core values and operations, businesses can become agents of positive change, driving innovation, and promoting sustainable practices that benefit both society and the environment.

CSR initiatives can take many forms, depending on the specific context and priorities of the company. Environmental sustainability is a major focus for many businesses, as they seek to reduce their carbon footprint, conserve resources, and minimize their impact on the environment. This might involve investing in renewable energy, implementing recycling programs, or developing eco-friendly products and packaging.

Ethical labor practices are another important aspect of CSR. This involves ensuring that workers are treated fairly, paid a living wage, and provided with safe and healthy working conditions. It also means respecting human rights, promoting diversity and inclusion, and avoiding any practices that exploit or harm workers or their communities.

Philanthropic giving is a common form of CSR, as businesses donate money or resources to charitable organizations and community initiatives. This can support a wide range of causes, from education and healthcare to poverty alleviation and disaster relief. Philanthropy can not only make a meaningful difference in the lives of others but also enhance a company's reputation and strengthen its relationships with stakeholders.

Community engagement is another important aspect of CSR. This involves partnering with local organizations, supporting community initiatives, and investing in the well-being of the communities where businesses operate. Community engagement can foster goodwill, build trust, and create a sense of shared purpose between businesses and their communities.

In recent years, there has been a growing trend towards integrating CSR into the core business strategy, rather than treating it as a separate philanthropic endeavor. This approach, known as "shared value," seeks to create economic value in a way that also creates value for society. By aligning business goals with social and environmental objectives, companies can create a win-win situation where both the company and society benefit.

The implementation of CSR initiatives requires a long-term commitment and a holistic approach. It is not simply about ticking boxes or complying with regulations; it is about embedding ethical and responsible practices into every aspect of the business. This requires leadership from the top, engagement from employees at all levels, and collaboration with stakeholders across the value chain.

The benefits of CSR are numerous and far-reaching. It can enhance a company's reputation, attract and retain top talent, improve customer loyalty, and increase profitability. It can also contribute to a more sustainable and equitable world, addressing social and environmental challenges and creating a positive impact on communities and the planet.

ᐯᐯᐯ

The most precious gifts we can give are those that come from the heart. A kind word, a listening ear, a helping hand—these are the gifts that truly make a difference in the lives of others.

♥♥♥

SEVENTEEN
GLOBAL ALTRUISM

Global altruism, the selfless concern for the well-being of others regardless of geographical boundaries, is a testament to the interconnectedness of humanity and our shared responsibility to create a more just and equitable world. It is a recognition that our actions, no matter where we live or what our circumstances may be, can have a ripple effect that extends far beyond our own communities. Global altruism transcends national borders, cultural differences, and socio-economic disparities, uniting us in a common cause to alleviate suffering, promote well-being, and build a more sustainable future for all.

At its core, global altruism is driven by empathy and compassion. It is the ability to see beyond our own immediate concerns and to recognize the struggles and aspirations of others around the world. It is the understanding that our actions, both individually and collectively, have consequences that extend far beyond our own borders. When we embrace global altruism, we acknowledge our shared humanity and our responsibility to care for one another, regardless of where we live or what our circumstances may be.

Global altruism can manifest in various ways. It can involve donating to international aid organizations, volunteering for global projects, advocating for human rights, supporting fair trade initiatives, or simply raising awareness about global issues. It can also involve making conscious choices in our daily lives, such as reducing our carbon footprint, supporting sustainable businesses, and consuming ethically sourced products.

The impact of global altruism is far-reaching. It can provide essential resources and support to communities in need, empowering them to overcome poverty, disease, and conflict. It can also foster cultural exchange and understanding, promoting peace and cooperation between nations. By working together across borders, we can address global challenges such as climate change, inequality, and social injustice, creating a more sustainable and equitable future for all.

The rise of technology and globalization has made it easier than ever for individuals to engage in global altruism. Online platforms and social media have connected people from all corners of the world, enabling us to share information, raise funds, and mobilize support for causes we care about. This interconnectedness has created a global community of altruists, who are working together to create positive change on a global scale.

However, global altruism also faces significant challenges. The sheer scale and complexity of global issues can be overwhelming, making it difficult to know where to start or how to make a meaningful impact. Cultural differences, political tensions, and economic disparities can also create barriers to collaboration and understanding. Moreover, there is a risk of paternalism and neocolonialism, where well-intentioned efforts to help can inadvertently perpetuate power imbalances and undermine local agency.

To overcome these challenges, global altruism must be grounded in humility, respect, and a willingness to learn from others. It must prioritize collaboration and partnership, recognizing that local communities are best equipped to understand their own needs and develop sustainable solutions. It must also be mindful of power dynamics and strive to empower local actors, rather than imposing solutions from outside.

One of the most promising approaches to global altruism is the concept of effective altruism. This movement advocates for using evidence and reason to determine the most effective ways to help others, maximizing the impact of our charitable giving. Effective altruists use rigorous analysis and data to identify the most pressing problems and the most effective interventions, focusing their resources on areas where they can make the biggest difference.

Another important aspect of global altruism is the recognition of the interconnectedness of social, economic, and environmental issues. Addressing global challenges requires a holistic approach that takes into account the complex interactions between these different factors. For example, poverty is often linked to environmental degradation, as impoverished communities are more vulnerable to the effects of climate change and resource depletion. By addressing these interconnected issues in a coordinated way, we can create a more sustainable and equitable future for all.

Global altruism is a powerful force for good in the world. It is a testament to the inherent goodness of humanity and our capacity for compassion, empathy, and generosity. By embracing global altruism, we can create a world where everyone has the opportunity to thrive, regardless of their nationality, ethnicity, or socioeconomic status. The challenges are many, but the rewards are even greater. As we move forward into an increasingly interconnected world, let us embrace the spirit of global altruism and work together to create a brighter future for all.

ppp

Giving is not a sacrifice; it is an investment in our own happiness and well-being. When we give to others, we not only uplift their spirits but also nourish our own souls.

ᐯᐯᐯ

EIGHTEEN

THE FUTURE OF GIVING

The future of giving is poised for a profound transformation, driven by a convergence of factors that are reshaping the landscape of philanthropy and social impact. As our world grapples with complex challenges such as climate change, inequality, and social unrest, the traditional models of giving are being challenged and reimagined. A new era of giving is emerging, one that is more inclusive, collaborative, and impact-oriented, leveraging technology, data, and a growing awareness of interconnectedness to create a more just and equitable world.

One of the most significant trends shaping the future of giving is the democratization of philanthropy. In the past, giving was often seen as the domain of the wealthy and privileged. However, the rise of crowdfunding platforms, online giving tools, and social media has made it easier than ever for individuals from all walks of life to contribute to causes they care about. This democratization is empowering a new generation of givers, who are more diverse, tech-savvy, and impact-oriented than their predecessors.

These new givers are not content with simply writing a check and walking away. They want to be actively involved in the causes they support, to see tangible results, and to hold organizations accountable for their impact. This demand for transparency and accountability is driving a shift towards more impact-driven philanthropy, where donors are increasingly focused on measuring and evaluating the effectiveness of their giving.

Technology is playing a pivotal role in this shift. Data analytics, artificial intelligence, and blockchain technology are being used to track the impact of donations, identify areas of greatest need, and optimize the allocation of resources. This data-driven approach to giving is enabling philanthropists to make more informed decisions, invest in solutions that have a proven track record of success, and measure the real-world impact of their contributions.

Another key trend shaping the future of giving is the growing emphasis on collaboration and partnership. In the past, philanthropy was often characterized by a top-down approach, with large foundations and wealthy individuals dictating the terms of their giving. However, there is a growing recognition that complex social and environmental challenges cannot be solved by any single actor.

Collaboration is becoming increasingly important, as philanthropists, nonprofits, businesses, and governments work together to address shared challenges. This collaborative approach is leading to more innovative and effective solutions, as stakeholders leverage their diverse skills, resources, and perspectives to create a greater impact.

The rise of impact investing, a form of investment that seeks to generate both financial return and social or environmental impact, is another example of the growing collaboration between the private and philanthropic sectors. Impact investors are increasingly investing in companies and projects that address social and environmental challenges, such as affordable housing, renewable energy, and sustainable agriculture. This convergence of finance and philanthropy is creating a new paradigm for social impact, where investors can generate both profit and purpose.

The future of giving is also being shaped by a growing awareness of interconnectedness. In a world that is increasingly interconnected, our actions have a ripple effect on others, both near and far. This recognition is leading to a greater emphasis on global giving, as philanthropists seek to address challenges that transcend national borders.

Furthermore, there is a growing recognition of the importance of systemic change. Addressing the root causes of poverty, inequality, and environmental degradation requires more than just individual acts of charity. It requires a systemic approach that addresses the underlying social, economic, and political structures that perpetuate these problems.

The future of giving is not without its challenges. Economic uncertainty, political polarization, and the rise of misinformation are just a few of the obstacles that could hinder progress. However, the potential for positive change is immense. By embracing new technologies, fostering collaboration, and focusing on impact, we can create a future where giving is more inclusive, effective, and transformative than ever before.

In this new era of giving, every individual has the power to make a difference. Whether through small acts of kindness, volunteering our time and skills, or investing in solutions that create lasting change, we can all contribute to a more just, equitable, and sustainable world.

 providedividedivided

Let us celebrate the diversity of giving, recognizing that every contribution, no matter how small, has the power to create positive change. Whether it is through volunteering, donating, or simply spreading kindness, we can all make a difference.

❥❥❥

NINETEEN

PERSONAL GROWTH THROUGH GIVING

Giving, in its many forms, is not just a transaction between individuals or an act of charity. It is a catalyst for profound personal growth, a transformative experience that ripples through our lives, enriching our hearts, expanding our minds, and awakening our spirits to a deeper sense of connection and purpose. When we give, we open ourselves up to a world of possibilities, where compassion, empathy, and gratitude intertwine to create a tapestry of personal transformation.

At its core, giving is an act of selflessness, a conscious choice to put the needs of others before our own. This act of selflessness can be a powerful antidote to the ego-driven tendencies that often dominate our lives. By shifting our focus from self-interest to the well-being of others, we break free from the limitations of our ego and tap into a deeper wellspring of compassion and generosity.

Giving also fosters a sense of empathy, the ability to understand and share the feelings of others. When we give, we step outside of our own perspectives and experiences, recognizing the shared humanity that binds us all. We see the world through the eyes of others, understanding their struggles, joys, and hopes. This expanded perspective can lead to greater compassion, tolerance, and acceptance, both towards ourselves and others.

Furthermore, giving can be a powerful tool for cultivating gratitude. When we recognize the abundance in our own lives and the opportunity to share it with others, we develop a deeper sense of appreciation for all that we have been given. This gratitude, in turn, can lead to increased happiness, resilience, and a more positive outlook on life. Studies have shown that individuals who regularly practice gratitude experience a wide range of benefits, including improved physical and mental health, stronger relationships, and greater overall life satisfaction.

Giving also has a profound impact on our sense of purpose and meaning. When we contribute to the well-being of others, we feel a sense of connection to something larger than ourselves. We realize that our actions have a ripple effect, impacting not only the lives of those we directly help but also the communities and systems in which we live. This sense of purpose can be incredibly empowering, motivating us to continue giving and contributing to the world in meaningful ways.

The act of giving can also challenge us to confront our own limitations and fears. When we step outside of our comfort zones and offer our time, resources, or expertise to others, we may encounter situations that test our patience, compassion, and resilience. However, these challenges can also be opportunities for growth, allowing us to develop new skills, overcome obstacles, and discover hidden strengths within ourselves.

Moreover, giving can be a source of profound joy and fulfillment. When we witness the positive impact of our actions on the lives of others, we experience a sense of satisfaction and purpose that is difficult to replicate through other means. This joy of giving can be contagious, inspiring us to continue giving and creating a ripple effect of positivity that spreads throughout our communities and beyond.

The personal growth that comes from giving is not limited to a single act or experience. It is an ongoing process that evolves and deepens over time. As we continue to give, we develop a greater capacity for empathy, compassion, and gratitude. We also gain a deeper understanding of ourselves, our values, and our place in the world. This personal growth can manifest in countless ways, from increased self-confidence and self-worth to a greater sense of purpose and meaning in life.

The path of giving is not always easy. It requires us to confront our own selfishness, fears, and insecurities. It challenges us to step outside of our comfort zones and embrace vulnerability. However, the rewards of this journey are immeasurable. By embracing the spirit of giving, we not only transform the lives of others, but we also embark on a profound journey of personal growth and transformation. We discover that giving is not just an act of kindness, but a pathway to a more meaningful, fulfilling, and compassionate life.

ppp

Giving is a reflection of our values, a testament to our belief in the interconnectedness of all beings. By giving generously, we affirm our commitment to creating a more just, equitable, and compassionate world.

ᐅᐅᐅ

TWENTY
INSPIRING STORIES OF ALTRUISM

The tapestry of human history is interwoven with threads of altruism, the selfless concern for the well-being of others that transcends self-interest and shines a light on the inherent goodness of humankind. These stories, often unsung and unheralded, serve as beacons of inspiration, reminding us of the transformative power of compassion, generosity, and the indomitable human spirit.

One such story is that of Irena Sendler, a Polish social worker who risked her life during World War II to rescue over 2,500 Jewish children from the Warsaw Ghetto. Under the guise of a nurse, she smuggled children out in ambulances, suitcases, and even coffins, providing them with false identities and placing them in safe homes. Her courage and selflessness saved countless lives and demonstrated the power of individual action in the face of overwhelming evil.

Another inspiring story is that of Malala Yousafzai, a Pakistani activist who, at the age of 15, was shot in the head by the Taliban for speaking out against the denial of education for girls. Despite facing death threats, she continued to advocate for girls' education, becoming the youngest Nobel Peace Prize laureate in history. Her unwavering determination and courage have inspired millions around the world and sparked a global movement for girls' education.

The story of Mahatma Gandhi, the Indian leader who championed nonviolent resistance as a means to achieve social and political change, is another testament to the power of altruism. Through his philosophy of Satyagraha, Gandhi inspired a nation to rise up against colonial rule and achieve independence. His unwavering commitment to nonviolence, compassion, and social justice continues to inspire activists and leaders around the world.

In the realm of science and medicine, the story of Dr. Jonas Salk, the developer of the polio vaccine, exemplifies altruism. When his vaccine was proven effective, Salk refused to patent it, choosing instead to make it freely available to the world. His selfless act saved countless lives and demonstrated that scientific innovation can be driven by a desire to serve humanity rather than by personal gain.

The story of Nelson Mandela, the South African anti-apartheid revolutionary who spent 27 years in prison for his activism, is a powerful testament to the transformative power of forgiveness and reconciliation. Upon his release, Mandela chose to lead his country not with vengeance, but with reconciliation, working tirelessly to heal the wounds of apartheid and build a more just and equitable society. His leadership and his unwavering commitment to forgiveness have inspired millions around the world and continue to serve as a beacon of hope in a world often marred by conflict and division.

These are just a few of the countless stories of altruism that have shaped our world. They remind us that even in the face of adversity, there are individuals who choose to act with compassion, generosity, and selflessness. Their actions inspire us, challenge us, and remind us of the inherent goodness that resides within each of us.

In a world that often seems focused on self-interest and material gain, these stories of altruism offer a ray of hope. They demonstrate that we are not powerless in the face of suffering and injustice, and that our individual actions can make a real difference in the lives of others. By embracing the spirit of altruism, we can create a world that is more compassionate, just, and equitable for all.

The legacy of these altruistic individuals lives on, not just in the history books, but in the hearts and minds of those they inspired. Their stories remind us that we all have the capacity for greatness, for compassion, and for making a positive impact on the world. By embracing altruism as a way of life, we can tap into our own inherent goodness and create a ripple effect of positive change that will extend far beyond our own lifetimes.

ppp

In the tapestry of life, giving is the golden thread that connects us all. It is the essence of our humanity, the source of our greatest joy, and the key to a more fulfilling and meaningful life.

♥♥♥

TWENTY-ONE
ALTRUISTIC ALCHEMY: A SUMMARY

The transformative power of giving is an undeniable force that shapes individuals, communities, and the world at large. It is an act of selflessness that transcends personal gain, driven by empathy, compassion, and a deep-seated desire to make a positive impact. Giving, in its many forms, is a catalyst for profound change, creating a ripple effect that touches the lives of both the giver and the receiver.

The essence of altruistic alchemy lies in the understanding that giving is not merely a transaction but a transformational process. It is a conscious choice to share our resources, time, and talents with others, not out of obligation, but out of a genuine desire to uplift and empower. This act of generosity, when practiced consistently and intentionally, can lead to profound personal growth, fostering empathy, compassion, gratitude, and a deeper sense of connection to the world around us.

Listening, an often-overlooked aspect of giving, is a crucial element in this alchemical process. True listening involves a deep engagement with the speaker, an openness to their experience, and a willingness to receive their message with an open heart and mind. It is an act of generosity that validates the speaker's existence and fosters a sense of connection and trust. The power of listening extends far beyond individual interactions, transforming communities, healing relationships, and bridging divides between cultures and nations.

Volunteering, the selfless offering of one's time and energy to a cause greater than oneself, is another powerful form of giving. It is an investment in our shared humanity, a testament to our interconnectedness, and a pathway to personal growth and fulfillment. Volunteering not only benefits the recipients of our service but also enriches our own lives by broadening our perspectives, deepening our empathy, and fostering a sense of purpose and meaning.

Giving without expectation is perhaps the purest form of altruism. It is a selfless act that transcends the desire for recognition or reward, flowing from a place of genuine compassion and a desire to alleviate suffering. When we give without expectation, we liberate ourselves from the shackles of attachment and the burden of reciprocity, experiencing a profound sense of joy, peace, and interconnectedness.

The gift of knowledge is another invaluable form of giving. Knowledge is not merely an accumulation of facts and figures; it is a dynamic force that encompasses wisdom, understanding, and the ability to apply what we learn to create positive change. By sharing our knowledge with others, we empower them to make informed decisions, solve problems, and create a better future for themselves and their communities.

Generosity in action is the embodiment of compassion, a tangible manifestation of our interconnectedness, and a testament to the inherent goodness of the human spirit. It is a force that transcends boundaries, unites communities, and creates a ripple effect of positive change that can transform lives and uplift entire societies. Generosity in action can take many forms, from small acts of kindness to grand philanthropic endeavors, and its impact is far-reaching.

Cultivating a giving mindset is essential for creating a culture of generosity and compassion. It involves a shift in perspective from scarcity to abundance, from self-interest to empathy, and from isolation to interconnectedness. By fostering a giving mindset, we can create a ripple effect of positivity, inspiring others to follow suit and contributing to a more equitable and harmonious world.

Gratitude plays a crucial role in cultivating a giving mindset. When we take the time to appreciate the abundance in our own lives, we are more likely to feel a sense of generosity towards others. Gratitude also has a profound impact on our well-being, increasing happiness, resilience, and overall life satisfaction.

Community building through giving is a powerful way to strengthen social bonds, foster resilience, and promote a sense of belonging. When giving is embedded within a community, it creates a culture of reciprocity and mutual support, empowering individuals to contribute to the collective well-being and create a more just and equitable society.

Giving as a family is a transformative experience that enriches the lives of all involved. It strengthens family bonds, imparts values such as empathy and compassion, and creates lasting memories. By giving together, families create a ripple effect of positivity throughout the community, inspiring others to follow suit and contributing to a more compassionate and connected society.

Sustainable giving is a philosophy and practice that recognizes the importance of balancing generosity with longevity. It involves creating systems and structures that support ongoing generosity while avoiding burnout and depletion. By prioritizing self-care, setting boundaries, and practicing mindfulness, givers can ensure that their generosity is sustainable in the long run.

Corporate social responsibility (CSR) is a vital component of modern business practice, demonstrating a commitment to society and the environment beyond the traditional profit-driven model. By integrating CSR into their core values and operations, businesses can improve their reputation and bottom line while contributing to a more sustainable and equitable future.

The future of giving is bright, with new technologies, collaborative approaches, and a growing awareness of interconnectedness shaping the landscape of philanthropy and social impact. This new era of giving is more inclusive, effective, and transformative than ever before, empowering individuals and communities to create a more just, equitable, and sustainable world.

Altruistic alchemy, the transformative power of giving, is a force that resides within each of us. By embracing this power, we can unlock our capacity for compassion, generosity, and connection, creating a ripple effect of positive change that extends far beyond our individual lives. As we embark on this journey of giving, let us remember that every act of kindness, no matter how small, has the potential to transform lives and create a brighter future for all.

ﭢﭢﭢ

Citation And References

This book represents the culmination of extensive research and meticulous analysis, incorporating a diverse range of sources, including numerous books, scholarly studies, and personal experiences. Additionally, I have scoured various websites to gather relevant information and data essential for the compilation of this work. I have taken every precaution to ensure the accuracy of the information presented and have diligently cited all sources to acknowledge their contributions.

Despite these efforts, the possibility of inadvertent errors remains. I deeply value the insights of my readers and appreciate any feedback that can help identify and rectify such inaccuracies. I encourage you to bring any discrepancies to my attention.

Your feedback is not only welcome but crucial, as it will aid in correcting current editions and enhancing the content of future ones. I am committed to maintaining the highest standards of accuracy and reliability in my work and thank you for your support and understanding.

Additionally, I firmly uphold the principle of freedom of speech and expression as guaranteed under Article 19(1)(a) of the Constitution of India, and I respect the diverse viewpoints and expressions of all readers.

ᐟᐟᐟ

Other Books Of The Author

1. Empowering Minds: A Journey into Women's Self-Discovery and Power
2. The Dynamics of Motivation: Catalyzing Thought into Action
3. Meditation and Mental Well Being: The Path to Inner Peace and Clarity
4. The Psychology of Child Education: Nurturing Future Generations
5. Ethical Enlightenment: A Modern Guide to Living with Integrity
6. Voices of Empowerment: Stories of Women Rising Against Odds
7. Social Psychology in Everyday Life: Understanding Human Connections
8. The Essence of Motivational Speaking: Inspiring Change in Others
9. Balancing Acts: Women, Work, and the Will to Lead
10. Guiding with Grace: Raising Children with Compassion and Awareness
11. The Power of Positive Aging: Embracing Life After Fifty
12. Building Resilient Communities: Social Work in Action
13. The Ethical Educator: Principles for Teaching and Learning
14. From Insight to Impact: Social Psychology for a Better World
15. The Ethics of Empathy: A Guide to Ethical Living
16. The Science of Empowering the Self: Navigating Life's Challenges with Psychological Wisdom
17. The Mindful Conscious Leader: Meditation Techniques for Modern Management
18. Pioneering Spirit: Women's Pathways to Leadership and Empowerment
19. Feeling to Healing: The Role of Emotional Intelligence in Child Development
20. Transformative Talks and Words of Inspiration: Insights into Motivational Oratory

21. Green Ethics: A Path to Sustainable Living
22. Spiritual Integrity: Navigating Life with Moral Compassion
23. Clean Living, Clean Society: The Ethics of Cleanliness
24. Patriotic Spirits: Building a Nation on Positive Attitudes
25. Innovative Integrity & Vibrant Visions: The Ethical and Entrepreneurial Spirit of Gujarat
26. Youthful Visions, Endless Possibilities: Inspiring Ethics and Motivation in Children
27. Living Your Legacy: How to Motivate Others by Living Your Values
28. Secret of Healing Conversations: Ethical Practices in Counselling and Therapy
29. Creative Kindness: Crafting a Life of Compassion and Creativity
30. The Power of Appreciation: How Gratitude Can Transform Your Relationships
31. Bhagavad-Gita: Messages
32. Science of Art: The New Frontier of Fashion Modernism
33. Vivekananda's Virtues: A Blueprint for Modern Living
34. Empower Her: Navigating the Path to Women's Entrepreneurship
35. The Boundless Classroom: Innovations in Global Education
36. The Language of Leadership: Communicating with Authenticity and Impact
37. The Warrior's Mantra: Deciphering the Hanuman Chalisa
38. Echoes of Empathy: Transformative Stories of Social Service
39. Artful Living: Cultivating Creativity in Your Daily Routine
40. Finding Your Why: Discovering Your Passions and Charting Your Course
41. The Role of Social Media in Shaping Self-Esteem and Interpersonal Relationships among Adolescents
42. Karma's Tapestry: Weaving a Life of Selfless Service
43. Altruistic Alchemy: Transforming Lives Through Giving
44. The Blueprint of Pro-Activeness and Productivity: Crafting Habits for Success
45. The Simplicity with Grounded Wisdom: Embracing Authenticity

in a Complex World

46. Secret of Solopreneur's Odyssey: Navigating the Path to Self-Employment
47. Exploring Tapestry of Peace: Global Perspectives on Harmony
48. The Art and Actions of Connection: Mastering Communication for Impact
49. She Governs and at the Helm: Strategies for Political Empowerment
50. Rising Above and Rising with Grace: A Woman's Roadmap to Career Mastery
51. The Effect of Networking & Connectedness: Building Strategic Alliances for Women
52. Beyond his Barriers: Women Thriving in Male-Dominated Fields
53. Secret of Inner Compass: Navigating Life with Intuition
54. Creative & Pro-Active Muses: A Celebration of Women in the Arts
55. Unburdened: The Art of Releasing the Past
56. Amplified Voices: Speeches of Women that Astonished the World
57. Secret of Manifesting Dreams: A Woman's Guide to Intentional Living
58. Ethics and Value Based Education: Reimagining Japan's School System
59. The Moral Compass Curriculum: A Holistic Approach
60. Tech with Heart: Integrating Ethics into Digital Learning
61. Honoring Virtue: Recognizing Ethical Excellence in Education
62. Raising Good Humans: A Guide to Character Development
63. The Spark Within: Nurturing Creativity in Children
64. The Teenager Whisperer: Navigating Adolescence with Grace
65. Igniting a Passion for Learning: Inspiring Lifelong Curiosity
66. The Habit Lab: Cultivating Positive Behaviors in Children
67. Seeds of Empathy: Fostering Compassion in Young Hearts
68. The Reading Revolution: Inspiring a Love of Books in Children
69. The Learning Brain: Unlocking the Secrets of Student Success
70. Teaching for All: Differentiated Instruction Strategies
71. The Time Alchemist: Mastering Time Management for Peak Performance

Bhajan
101. Pilgrimage of the Soul: Spiritual Journeys in India

ÞÞÞ

Contact

Dr. Minakshi Bansal
Social Activist
Ahmedabad, Gujarat, Bharat
minakshiindiag20@yahoo.com

❥❥❥

|| LOKAHA SAMASTHAHA SUKHINO BHAVANTU ||

• 141 •